Dear Parent:

Congratulations! Your child is taking the first steps on an exciting journey. The destination? Independent reading!

STEP INTO READING® will help your child get there. The program offers books at five levels that accompany children from their first attempts at reading to reading success. Each step includes fun stories, fiction and nonfiction, and colorful art. There are also Step into Reading Sticker Books, Step into Reading Math Readers, and Step into Reading Phonics Readers— a complete literacy program with something to interest every child.

Learning to Read, Step by Step!

Ready to Read   Preschool–Kindergarten
• big type and easy words • rhyme and rhythm • picture clues
For children who know the alphabet and are eager to begin reading.

Reading with Help   Preschool–Grade 1
• basic vocabulary • short sentences • simple stories
For children who recognize familiar words and sound out new words with help.

Reading on Your Own   Grades 1–3
• engaging characters • easy-to-follow plots • popular topics
For children who are ready to read on their own.

Reading Paragraphs   Grades 2–3
• challenging vocabulary • short paragraphs • exciting stories
For newly independent readers who read simple sentences with confidence.

Ready for Chapters   Grades 2–4
• chapters • longer paragraphs • full-color art
For children who want to take the plunge into chapter books but still like colorful pictures.

STEP INTO READING® is designed to give every child a successful reading experience. The grade levels are only guides. Children can progress through the steps at their own speed, developing confidence in their reading, no matter what their grade.

Remember, a lifetime love of reading starts with a single step!

For Amy and Sarah
—J.D.

For Hiroshi Miyazaki
—D.D.

Photo credits: cover, from the book *Full Moon*, published by Alfred A. Knopf, a division of Random House, Inc., © 1999 Michael Light; pp. 7, 25, 31, 43, courtesy of NASA; p. 19, White House Photo Collection, John F. Kennedy Library.

Text copyright © 1989 by Judy Donnelly. Illustrations copyright © 1989 by Dennis Davidson. All rights reserved under International and Pan-American Copyright Conventions. Published in the United States by Random House Children's Books, a division of Random House, Inc., New York, and simultaneously in Canada by Random House of Canada Limited, Toronto.

www.stepintoreading.com

Educators and librarians, for a variety of teaching tools, visit us at
www.randomhouse.com/teachers

Library of Congress Cataloging-in-Publication Data
Donnelly, Judy.
Moonwalk : the first trip to the moon / by Judy Donnelly ; illustrated by Dennis Davidson.
    p.   cm. — (Step into reading. A step 5 book)
SUMMARY: Narrates the preparations and activities which culminated in man's first landing on the moon in July 1969.
ISBN 0-394-82457-1 (trade) — ISBN 0-394-92457-6 (lib. bdg.)
1. Space flight to the moon—Juvenile literature.   2. Project Apollo (U.S.)—Juvenile literature.
[1. Space flight to the moon.   2. Project Apollo (U.S.)]
I. Davidson, Dennis, ill.   II. Title.   III. Series: Step into reading. Step 5 book.
TL799.M6D66 2003 629.45'4—dc21   2002153804

Printed in the United States of America   38 37 36 35 34 33 32 31 30 29

STEP INTO READING, RANDOM HOUSE, and the Random House colophon are registered trademarks of Random House, Inc.

MOONWALK

The First Trip to the Moon

By Judy Donnelly

Illustrated by Dennis Davidson

— with photographs —

Random House 🏠 New York

1

Moon Launch

July 16, 1969. Cape Kennedy, Florida.

A huge white rocket towers against the blue sky. It is thirty-six stories high. It weighs over six million pounds. It is called the *Saturn V.* It is the biggest, most powerful rocket ever built.

Today it is going to make the dream of centuries come true. It will send three men where no human being has ever been before. To the moon!

A few miles away almost a million people crowd the highways and beaches. Small boats full of excited people dot the ocean. They have all come to see the launch. People are not allowed any closer. The danger of an explosion is too great.

Around the planet millions more people are watching their television screens. Everyone wants to share in the longest, most incredible voyage in history.

As launch time approaches, three astronauts in gleaming white spacesuits walk toward the huge rocket. Their names are Neil Armstrong, Edwin "Buzz" Aldrin, and Michael Collins.

The men get into an elevator. They ride up to the top of the launch tower. There, at the very tip of the rocket, a spacecraft is waiting. It is called *Apollo 11*.

Soon the astronauts are inside the cramped spacecraft, strapped tightly to their seats. They are excited and tense.

For many months they have prepared for this journey. They know every inch of the spacecraft. Every detail of the flight plan. They are as ready as anyone can be to go

Apollo 11 astronauts Neil Armstrong, left, Michael Collins, center, and Edwin "Buzz" Aldrin, right. All three men are expert pilots, but each has been in space only once before.

into the unknown. Now their lives will depend on nine million bits of machinery working exactly right.

The astronauts wait quietly. Then over their radios they hear the voice of mission control wish them good luck and Godspeed. It is time. Time to shoot for the moon. The countdown begins: "10, 9, 8, 7, 6, 5, 4, 3, 2, 1, 0...liftoff!"

The rocket rises into the air with an ear-splitting roar. It climbs higher and higher, trailing smoke and fire.

Miles away people watch in awe. They are deafened by the noise. The ground shakes under them. The rocket looks like a streak of flame. Can anyone ride in it and survive?

Inside the *Apollo* the astronauts are shoved back into their seats. The spacecraft jerks and rattles and sways. The men never look away from their controls. So far, so good.

The first rocket stage drops away. Then the second. The ride gets rougher as the third stage takes over.

Less than twelve minutes have passed since the launch. But the *Apollo* is already more than one hundred miles away from Earth. Through their windows the astronauts can see a vast stretch of their planet—land, sea, and clouds.

The men are weightless now. They float about the cabin. They will orbit Earth one and a half times while they make a last check of all systems. Then they will set off on a straight course for the moon.

Everything is working perfectly. The astronauts strap themselves back into their seats. Now they fire the engine that will send them to their destination. There is no turning back. The *Apollo* goes faster and faster—almost 25,000 miles an hour.

Next stop…the moon.

2

How Do You Get to the Moon?

For thousands of years people dreamed of traveling to the moon.

Until a few hundred years ago people weren't even sure what the moon was. They watched it gleam in the darkness. They saw it change its shape and sometimes disappear. Was it a god or goddess? Was it the home of strange, magical beings? Was it a world like our own? It seemed there was no way to find out except by going there.

People had some unusual ideas about how to do that. One man thought a giant spout of water could lift a ship and send it up to the moon. Others thought birds were the

answer. Why couldn't someone climb on the
back of a big eagle? Or train swans to carry a
passenger to the moon in a basket?

The moon was such a mystery that many people came to believe it had magical powers. Dangerous powers. Don't sleep in the moonlight, they warned. Never plant when the moon is full. Step out under a full moon and you could go mad. Or turn into a werewolf!

The invention of the telescope in the 1600s gave people a better idea of what the moon was really like. They saw mountains and craters and valleys on the moon. They made out dark areas that they thought were oceans and seas. They even gave them names like the Sea of Clouds and the Sea of Tranquility. Later, when telescopes improved, scientists decided the dark areas were really dry plains. But the names stayed.

Telescopes taught people a little more about the moon. But that didn't get them any closer.

As the years passed there were other

inventions. In the 1800s explorers went floating high over the countryside in hot-air balloons. The telegraph let people send messages over many miles in just a few seconds.

Science was making impossible dreams come true. This gave a writer named Jules Verne an idea. In 1865 he wrote a book called *From the Earth to the Moon*. In it a spaceship was shot to the moon by a giant cannon! Verne was wrong about the cannon.

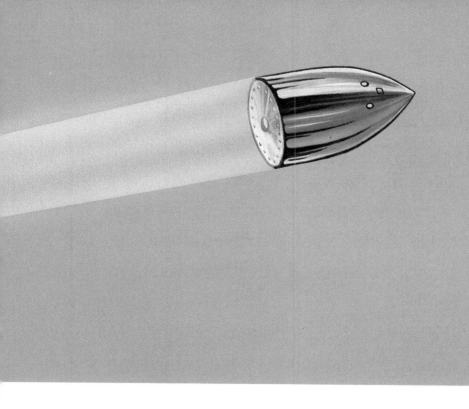

That would never work. But he was right about other things. Verne's imaginary ship was steered by rockets. People had been using small rockets for centuries, both as war weapons and for fireworks. But no one had ever thought of using rockets in space before.

Children from different parts of the world read Verne's book. They liked his idea of space travel and rockets. Some grew up to become scientists. In the 1920s and 1930s an

American scientist named Robert Goddard did important experiments with rockets. He even wrote a report that said rockets could reach the moon.

Scientists kept improving rockets. By the 1940s rockets could travel about 200 miles. They were used by Germany to bomb England in World War II. After the war, scientists tried to develop rockets for space travel. But the moon? That was still a distant dream.

Then, in 1961, something happened. President John F. Kennedy made a speech. He told the world that America would send a man to the moon before the 1960s ended. Going to the moon was no longer a dream. It was a goal.

Why did President Kennedy set this deadline? The reason had to do with another country—the Soviet Union. America had a space program. But the Soviet Union had a better one. It sent up the world's first satellite. Then

President John F. Kennedy (on the right) set America on a course for the moon.

it sent the first man into space. Newspapers said the two countries were in a space race and America was losing. President Kennedy decided there was one sure way to win—be first on the moon.

Kennedy had made a promise. But could America keep it?

By 1961 some rockets had flown a few hundred miles up into space. But the moon was almost a quarter of a *million* miles away!

A trip to the moon and back would take eight days. By 1961 only one American had even been up in space—and for only fifteen minutes!

Just aiming for the moon was a problem in itself. A rocket couldn't be aimed at where the moon was in the sky because the moon moves about 50,000 miles each day. Scientists would have to aim at an empty spot in space where the moon was *going to be* by the time the spacecraft got there. It would take some very careful figuring. If there was a mistake, the spacecraft would go off into space forever!

Was it safe to land on the moon? Many scientists thought the moon was covered with a layer of dust fifty feet deep. A spacecraft would be swallowed up in it!

Scientists needed answers. They decided to send robot spacecraft with cameras to the moon. They called them *probes*. Scientists tried but failed—twelve times! Sometimes the probes just fell back to Earth in flames. Two got as far as the moon, then missed it. Off they went into space—never to return. Suppose human beings had been on these flights?

A moon probe explodes just after liftoff.

It took three years before a probe finally landed on the moon. More probes followed. One even took the first pictures of the far side of the moon—the side that is never seen from Earth. The news was good. The ground seemed firm and solid. And even though there were huge mountains and craters and cliffs on the moon, there were also smooth, flat stretches that looked safe for a landing.

The moon might be safe for a spacecraft. But could a human being survive that long, long journey? And could a human being actually walk on the moon?

There was one way to find out. Train human beings to travel into black, unending space—and see what would happen to them.

3

Wanted: Astronauts

Who were these human guinea pigs? Who were these men who would risk their lives to explore space?

The first astronauts were pilots. They were the bravest, smartest, healthiest pilots the space program could find. Most of them had proved their courage as test pilots or fighter pilots during wartime.

Becoming an astronaut in the 1960s wasn't easy. Doctors weren't sure what a long spaceflight would do to the human body. So they gave the men all kinds of tests to be sure they could handle nearly anything. They left them in completely dark, sound-proof rooms for hours. They put them in rooms heated to 130 degrees. They blasted them with noise. They bounced them up and down. They spun them around and around.

Hundreds of top pilots applied for astronaut training. By 1964 only thirty men had been chosen.

It was dangerous and expensive to send astronauts up in space. So the training was done right here on Earth.

Scientists built a model of a spacecraft called a *simulator.* It had hundreds of dials and levers and lights and buttons and switches, just like the real thing. The astronauts could even see fake views of the moon and stars from the windows.

From the outside the *simulator* looked like a crazy jumble of boxes.

Inside, a simulator was an exact working model of an Apollo spacecraft. It gave astronauts a risk-free chance to practice spaceflight.

An astronaut sat inside. Suddenly a warning would flash. Engine failure! An air leak! The astronaut had to do the right thing to fix it—fast. He could always try again on the simulator. But a mistake in space could cost him his life.

Scientists wanted astronauts to get used to the crushing pressure that they would feel when a rocket blasted off and when it returned to Earth. So they came up with something called the *centrifuge*. The astronauts called it the wheel. It looked like an amusement-park ride, but it was no fun at all. The wheel whirled the astronaut around faster and faster. His chest would feel heavier and heavier. He would have trouble breathing and seeing. Sometimes he would even faint. Everyone hated the wheel.

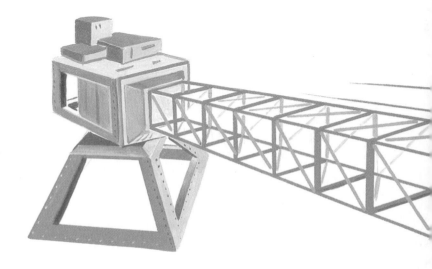

Scientists wanted to know what being weightless in space would do to astronauts. Only spaceflight could really answer the question. But astronauts needed to practice being weightless on Earth. Scientists found a way. An astronaut rode in the back of a jet plane. The jet would go into a steep climb and a dive. For about thirty seconds, during the dive, the astronaut would feel weightless. That wasn't much. But it was time enough to try eating and drinking and moving around.

An astronaut sits inside the ball of the *centrifuge.*

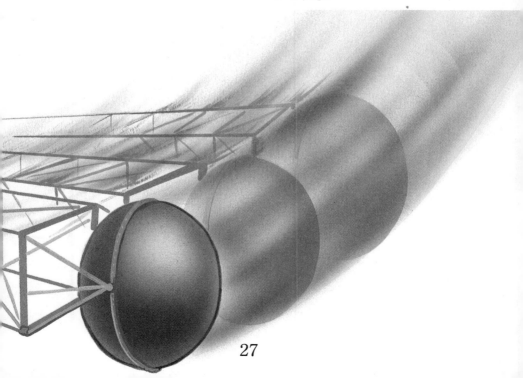

27

After hundreds of hours of ground training the astronauts got a chance at the real thing—spaceflight. Each launch was a big event. The risks were great, and the costs ran to millions of dollars. Most astronauts went up just once or twice.

These early trips were very important. The astronauts stayed up in space for longer and longer times. And they traveled closer and closer to the moon.

President Kennedy died in 1963. Still, everyone in the space program worked hard to meet the deadline that he had set—a trip to the moon by 1969. And they did it.

But when *Apollo 11* was finally launched, everyone knew the truth. No matter how much they had trained and tested and planned, something could still go wrong.

No one could be sure the astronauts would reach the moon. No one could be sure they would return safely to Earth.

Astronauts often risked their lives. Here one floats hundreds of miles above the earth to test whether human beings can survive in open space.

4

Destination Moon

July 16, 1969. Somewhere in space.

Apollo 11 is hurtling through black space. It is going more than six miles a second—faster than a bullet!

Inside, the astronauts—Armstrong, Aldrin, and Collins—feel as though they are hardly moving at all.

But through their windows they see Earth growing smaller and smaller. It is a beautiful sight. They can see the blue of the oceans, white clouds, and red deserts. And the earth is so bright! It is much brighter than the moon. The astronauts can even read by earthshine.

An actual photograph of Earth, taken from a spacecraft.

In three days they will reach their destination.

It is hard to keep track of time. Noon and midnight look the same because the sun never stops shining on the spacecraft. The side of the craft facing the sun could get dangerously hot. So the astronauts keep *Apollo* in a slow spin. It turns like meat on a barbecue spit.

At night the men sleep zipped up in floating hammocks. Each morning mission control radios to awaken them.

They fix special space meals. All the food has been dried and squeezed into plastic packets so that it won't float away. The men cook by squirting hot water from a kind of water pistol into the packets. Buzz Aldrin loves the shrimp. Mike Collins likes the chicken soup. But the peanut cubes? Bleh!

They have to watch out for spills. Droplets and crumbs would just float around the cabin. Even though they are careful, they still lose pencils and toothbrushes. And they bump into

Cooking dinner on board *Apollo 11*.

each other. There just isn't much room.

On July 19 the astronauts get their first closeup view of the moon. It no longer looks like a small, flat circle in the sky. It looks like an enormous ball! Armstrong says, "It's a view worth the price of the trip."

The moon is between the spacecraft and the sun. It blocks out the sun's light—except for a beautiful glow around the edges. Still, the men can see mountains, cliffs, and craters.

The surface looks very rough. Will they really be able to land on it?

On the next day it is time. Time to land on the moon.

The spacecraft is going to divide into two parts. Aldrin and Armstrong will head for the moon in one part—a landing craft called the *Eagle*. Mike Collins will stay behind in the other part—the command module. The command module is named *Columbia* for Christopher Columbus.

Aldrin says, "The *Eagle* has wings!" as the landing craft separates from the command ship.

Very carefully Aldrin and Armstrong climb into spacesuits with backpacks. They make sure all the fastenings are very tight. They will depend on their suits for many things. For air. For protection against the blistering heat of the sun. For radio contact with Earth. Without their suits they would die.

Then the two astronauts crawl into the *Eagle*. The landing craft separates from the command ship. And they are on their way.

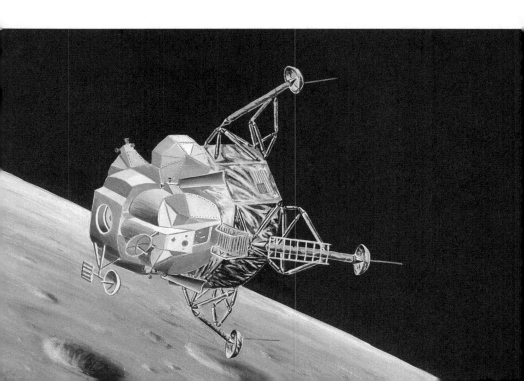

The *Eagle* drops closer and closer to the moon. This is a moment of great danger. Aldrin and Armstrong must land quickly because they have very little fuel. But if they come down too fast, they may crash.

The *Eagle* must land on smooth, flat ground. If it tips over, if a leg breaks—it will not be able to lift off. The two astronauts will be trapped on the moon forever. And they have enough air for only a single day.

The *Eagle* is almost on the surface. Suddenly Armstrong sees they are in trouble. They are about to land in a crater—full of huge boulders! Armstrong steers away. His fuel is almost gone. He has only seconds to find a better spot. He does it! And the *Eagle* touches down.

Armstrong's voice is heard all around Earth, almost a quarter-million miles away. "The *Eagle* has landed."

5

Moonwalk

Back at mission control people are clapping and cheering. The astronauts have made it! Up in the command module Collins says, "Fantastic!"

Soon comes the most exciting moment of all. Armstrong opens the hatch and steps down. His first words are, "That's one small step for a man, one giant leap for mankind."

He is standing on the moon.

It is a thrilling, almost unbelievable moment. For the first time a human being is on the moon looking back at Earth. And on Earth, across thousands of miles of star-studded space, people watch their television screens and share the adventure.

Aldrin joins Armstrong.

For a moment the men just look around them. It is beautiful and strange.

Nothing moves. There is no wind or weather. No sign of life anywhere.

Bright sunshine lights up the surface of the moon. But the sky is black. And way off in the distance hangs a tiny, shining blue-white Earth.

It is time to explore. Together the two astronauts walk into the gray-white world.

The ground is covered with a powdery dust. With almost every step they leave footprints—footprints on the moon! If no one comes to disturb them, they will stay just as they are for millions of years.

It is easy to walk, even in stiff, heavy spacesuits. Because of the moon's gravity, the men feel as if they weigh only sixty pounds. They take big, floating steps—they call them kangaroo hops. The astronauts can jump as high as twenty feet on the moon.

But neither man wants to try. Suppose he tears his spacesuit? He will die within seconds.

The astronauts take photographs. Then they set an American flag in the moon soil. It looks as though it is blowing in the breeze. That is only because thin wires have made it stiff.

Suddenly the two men get a surprise. Mission control tells them that the president of the United States, Richard Nixon, is on the telephone from the White House. He wants to congratulate them. It is certainly the longest long-distance call ever made!

Then the astronauts get back to their work. They collect moonrocks and moon dust. And they set up experiments. One will record any moonquakes. Others will help scientists learn more about the sun, the moon, and Earth. Some of the instruments will keep sending information to Earth for years to come.

The largest audience in television history watched an American flag planted on the moon.

Soon it is time to rejoin the *Columbia*. The *Eagle* must be as light as possible for liftoff. So the astronauts leave everything they don't need. Boots, backpacks, cameras, and a bundle of litter from the trip!

They leave special medals in memory of astronauts from both America and the Soviet Union who lost their lives in the space program.

And they leave behind an important message.

It says:

Here men from the planet Earth
first set foot upon the moon
July 1969
We came in peace for all mankind

In the *Columbia,* about sixty miles above the moon, Collins is waiting. While Armstrong and Aldrin were exploring, he has orbited the moon all alone, twenty-five times. Each time he passed to the far side, radio contact with other human beings was impossible. No other person has ever been so alone. What was going through his mind? Did he wish he could walk on the moon like the others? Yes, but he felt very lucky just to be along on the trip.

Now Collins is very nervous. He knows the *Eagle* must lift off and link up perfectly with his spacecraft for the return trip. If the liftoff fails, Collins won't be able to help. He will have to leave his friends behind—to die on the moon.

Aldrin and Armstrong know the risks they face. They fire the *Eagle*'s engine. The moon craft separates from its landing legs and rises up in a shower of sparks.

Soon the *Eagle* joins up with the *Columbia*. The three astronauts are back together—and on their way home!

Sixty hours later three giant parachutes set the spacecraft down onto the waves of the Pacific Ocean. Splashdown! A ship full of cheering sailors is waiting nearby. So is the president of the United States.

Everyone is thrilled to see the three

astronauts return all the way from the moon. But no one hugs them. No one even shakes their hands. Why? Everyone is afraid of moon germs!

Scientists are worried that the men might have brought back germs that could cause strange moon diseases. To be safe, Collins, Aldrin, and Armstrong put on germproof rubber suits. They stay in a germproof van. Everyone, even the president, congratulates them through a little window. So do their wives and children!

After three weeks the doctors are certain there are no moon germs, and the astronauts are free again. There are parades and celebrations for them all over America.

Next they make a trip to twenty-three countries around the world. And everywhere they go, people say, "*We* did it!" Everyone feels the success belongs not just to America but to all human beings.

And how do the astronauts feel to be back on Earth?

A surprising thing has happened to each of them. They have come back with a special feeling about our planet. They remember how it looked from the spacecraft—all shining and beautiful and very small in the black emptiness of space. They hope the people of Earth will take good care of it.

In the years to come, human beings will travel farther and farther into space. They will make wonderful discoveries. But we may find that the most perfect world in the universe is the one we know best. The planet Earth.